T0155095

BROKEN
FACE

RUSSELL THORNTON

THE
BROKEN
FACE

POEMS

HARBOUR
PUBLISHING

Harbour Publishing
P.O. Box 219, Madeira Park, BC, V0N 2H0
www.harbourpublishing.com

Edited by Silas White
Cover design by Anna Comfort O'Keeffe
Cover: Details from *Dynamism of a Man's Head*, Umberto Boccioni, 1913.
Text design by Mary White
Printed and bound in Canada

Harbour Publishing acknowledges the support of the Canada Council for the
Arts, which last year invested $153 million to bring the arts to Canadians
throughout the country. We also gratefully acknowledge financial support from
the Government of Canada and from the Province of British Columbia through
the BC Arts Council and the Book Publishing Tax Credit.

Library and Archives Canada Cataloguing in Publication

Thornton, Russell, author
    The broken face : poems / Russell Thornton.

Issued in print and electronic formats.
ISBN 978-1-55017-844-9 (paper).—ISBN 978-1-55017-845-6 (ebook)

    I. Title.

PS8589.H565B76 2018   C811'.54   C2018-903573-0
                                                 C2018-903574-9

There is the white fire that flames out of a man's face;
it hides the evidence of what it burns from beginning to end
repairing the man's broken face everywhere—
it imprisons itself in the man to try to see itself, it goes free
when the face breaks and the man must search and search for his face.

Contents

I

Scales	*11*
Screaming	*12*
A Man on Death Row	*13*
Open	*14*
Driving	*16*
Jail	*18*
Week-Old Son	*20*
Cell	*21*
Gunman	*24*
A Drop of Blood	*26*
The Chance	*28*

II

Water Makes Its Way	*31*
Soccer Ball	*32*
Teeth	*34*
Tying Shoes	*36*
Question	*37*
My Four-Year-Old Son and a Bicycle Pump	*38*
Copper Door	*40*
Dandelions	*42*
Picking Blackberries with My Daughter	*44*
Xmastime Dancing	*46*
Woolly Snow	*48*

III

The Shore	*51*
Bubble	*52*
Tiny Crabs	*53*

North Vancouver   54
When the Rain Comes   56
Cart Riders   58
Sirens   60
Aftermath   62
At Safeway   64
Stopping the Waves   66
Wildfire: Photos   68
Stroller   69
The Water and the Stone Trap   70

IV

Birthmark   73
Two Houses   74
A Dove   75
O God, Beast, Mystery, Come!   76
The Broken Face   78
Summer Vineyard, Naramata   80
The Finch, Questions and Answers   81
A Photograph   82
Girl on a Tire Swing   84
The Wound   86
Creating a Timeline   90
Change   92

Notes & Acknowledgements   93
About the Author   95

I

Scales

He is seven pounds, four ounces,
and cries alone on the steel base plate.

The argument for the prosecution—his pulse.
The argument for the defence—his pulse.

Screaming

A young son waking terrified, shrieking in the summer night heat wave.
The fearful neighbour hears him and calls the police.

I am not his father. I was lost and was led here through an instant.
I do not know where I come from. I do not know this room. I am here
      with a child

whose tears blur and brighten his staring eyes. I try to comfort him,
and he flails at me and fights me off. I see he is stranded here,

carrying with him nothing he understands, and it includes me.
He is an unknown carrier of unknown me, and has the face of a small
      wild animal.

You who do not know me, you who have put me here,
with no place to go back to or escape to, please take me up into your
      arms.

I know coolness will come only at the hour before dawn. Then just
      within the skull
of the baby will come the rippling of light. The window will hold the
      first full flames.

The old energy immense and hidden within the atom
will have dreamt a bonfire on a cold beach of space. The sun will arrive
      and circle

through the piled-high discarded furniture of the world in search of
      shelter
and rise and be the fire of the day with no address but a crib and a cry.

A Man on Death Row

Stone tablets smashed then re-carved every second in his eyes,
he shuffles down the corridor with his ankle shackles ringing.

He knows the contraction that stays and hardens into bars.
And how a brief kiss within a nucleus fastens the nothing to the nothing.

He knows from memory the deep fires of morning. They touch him
      completely.
And how the sun is straitjacketed in its life in his cells.

He knows the expansion that stays and opens on an endless wedding—
the father gives away the bride at the end of every ray of light.

Enormous levered energies—those of the distant hydro dam
sending the voice of God rushing into his system like the sounds of all
      the rivers

flowing with ceremony and heard by a single human being as by a
      multitude—
concentrate electricity and the sudden black ash of his Adam's apple,

thrill his windpipe. The immortal audience sees there the beauty
of his sentence. Odysseus is lashed to his mast, near insane in ecstasy.
      Christ

is fixed to the wood, the riven wrists and feet the narrowings
of hourglasses turning over and over again catching the warm blood.

At the appointed time he offers his charred heart, his hooded head and
      meat.
Whatever words he has uttered here, they are the vow that saves the law.

Open

Everywhere: *Open, Open.* Stores, banks. Stores, banks.
Gas stations. *Open, Open Later, Open.*
For as long as I can remember, I have thought about stealing.

Once I scoped out and robbed the Number Five Orange.
The storage cellar had a steel hatch at ground level
with an easily removable commercial padlock.

I shimmied down through the small square opening
and with the city police station a block away,
in perfect calm I hoisted cases of beer to an accomplice.

In the weeks after, I got drunk many times for free.
My most professionally carried out act of crime gone unnoticed,
I could not help it, I gave in, I told people—

drinking at the St. Alice in North Van,
bragging about the great cache in my car,
I ended up on the Capilano Reserve,

and I and two old school friends shared the last of the Labatt.
Out in the river in the dark, we gaffed coho,
laughing as we arrested pilgrim after silver pilgrim

beginning its ascent to the top of the canyon to spawn and die.
The tide was coming in, sea and river water
moving together, wrapping around me

where I stood in pants and shoes swaying, tottering. We gaffed.
We chucked salmon into the now-empty trunk.
I would take it home and eat it. They would take it home

and eat it, or sell it. We gaffed. The oncoming wild eyes
of the fish staring straight into the first rays of the late summer sun.
The angled mouths of the fish, the blackness: *Open, Open.*

Driving

I keep my headlights on, as recommended, even in daylight,
today and every day. In the night, when high beams strike my eyes,
I experience blind hate. Now I am walking across a street—

someone runs me down; I lie there fetal in the ticking glare.
They award me money, but I can never again run more than a few
    strides—
a dead leg, no spring in it. When I once ran races

and set records that stood for years. The steel screw and hinge
that had to be inserted in my knee now act as a transmitter and receiver
which communicate with me like a low-level deity; it sends an ache

the length of my leg alerting me to falling barometric pressure;
it signals me with my own yearning in the hour before rain—
now eternity will touch my entire skin at once. Now I ride

on a stationary bike at a rec centre gym for exactly thirty minutes,
my legs going around and around; I note the digits
indicating my achieved speed and distance. Today and every day.

I worry incessantly about the future, and my worry haunts me
like the past. Now I drive over a nail. At a repair shop, a workman
    informs me
he is not permitted to fix bald tires. Without my knowing it,

all four tires have lost almost all their treads. At any moment then,
on any icy or rain-slicked asphalt I might spin directionless, all my
    chances
gathered right there. And so I purchase quality new tires

that will take good hold of the road. I am vehicle-proud,
I am imitating a life, I am trying to do things right. Today and every day.
I take the wheel, click on the lights and shine them invisibly into the
      light.

Jail

A murder of crows stands along a power line,
and I hear nothing all morning but the cawing,
and see nothing but the shapes of blackness—
the sires who deal out death, and find and eat the dead—
and then I recall sitting naked hours in a chair
in a hot, bulb-glare-bright, urine-soaked cell.
Waking another time, face to a cement floor,
in a lock-up out of an old TV sitcom,
breathing in cleaning-bleach fumes, vomiting.
Striding proudly into a cell in North Vancouver—
the place I had always wanted to be.
Hometown RCMP jail. Smooth grey walls.
Pure white bowl. Steel ledge bed. I hear my heart muscle
contracting in rhythm as if working wings.
Almost hear it caw. Almost feel the valves,
the membranous doors allowing the blood
to flow in and not out, out and not in.
Know now my heart is the scavenger of my blood—
its one need is to fill its emptying hollow.
I have brought it to a barred concrete box
to clench, to unclench, and plead in this way
for blood to flow with force in through a door
to the son I am, and out through a door
to a father cawing down the corridor artery—
and back again to where sons and fathers
must begin and end, and meet in nothingness. Crows
fly off then up to the tops of power poles.
I want the caws and carcass-dripping beaks
to show me the way to no right or wrong,
good or bad, love or hate, to instruct me
in how there is nothing more than the hearts

of those judged to be lost, apart, punished.
I want to walk in the heart of the criminal,
the father and son who are free, the man
who holds within his core the life that beats
in a small bird or crow, and moves through a flower,
even as he is led away in the sun to be killed.

Week-Old Son

A man has come floundering late in the night
to stand alone at the shore of a sleeping infant's face.
The small pillow, the sheet, the mattress, the crib,

all the things in the bedroom rush into the black,
and the man stands in front of a wave arriving
bristling with froth like expiring white sparks,

and he kneels within his eyes. The man kneels
and is burning on sand, and a shout issues from him
hardly his own and not a sound anyone else can hear,

and not forming anything like a word. Whatever
has compelled him to come to this shore in the night,
whatever he regrets he has done or left undone,

he can never go back and be again the man he was,
he can never go find again his own father, mother.
He can do nothing, nothing other than kneel

and offer up what he is in the animal present,
a body a carrier of time as a star is
in its burning and shining for its fuel, and in doing this

call to the stars. If the infant wakes crying, and the man
reaches to him in love, even now he lives in no life
he can know, although his call to the stars is also a call

to his burning son. The brilliant, cold tide flows in
over the man's legs, the air from the far end of the ocean
runs its endless hand that is no hand across his brow.

Cell

I

I note the slat.
The small thin blanket.
The metal ledge bed.
The grey concrete.
The seatless toilet bowl.
The air-conditioned cold.
My fingertips
smelling of soap, ink.
The hourly checks
through the slat.
The feel of my arms
folded around me.
My calm as when
someone lets go,
freezing or drowning.
It will take me
until morning
to collect the particulars.

II

Down the corridor,
voices of others
I did not know
were here.
I need a fucking doctor.
I need
a fucking doctor.
Shut the fuck up.
A morning muffin
and juice box

through the slat.
The taste of my own spit.
The door opens.
I stand, and the flesh
of my face crumbles.
I am led out
to a courtroom
and a judge.

III

I speak the way
that people speak.
The same criminal
appears here
every hour.
As babies and the elderly
all look and act alike.
The evidence,
the judge says,
is in the loose cement
of your face, your arms
and legs and hands.
Yes, eye to eye
with him, I admit
I laid the concrete
blocks of four walls
to keep a secret
that I do not know.

IV

I invite you, I say,
to decide how to punish
what is left of me
and for how long.

I submit to you my skull
with its fixed stare.
Where I live within it
is an elsewhere
and is neither
day nor night,
it is no time.
The things you note
are to me opening slats.
I look through them
and see as far
into and out of a cell
as death and change
will take me.

Gunman

If he is somewhere near,
let him come to me. If he
is standing at a bookshelf
pretending to look at titles,
or sitting at a study table
turning pages, or walking in
through the main library door,
a rifle hidden inside his coat,
let him come to me. Little
kids are listening to a story,
adolescents are preparing
their school assignments,
people are typing at public
desktop computers. Not
far away, TV cameras
are ready. Everywhere,
hand-held devices are ready.
Building security officers
are ready. I have been ready
as long as I can remember.

Let him come to me. Let him
look a long time into my face
as he raises his weapon
and aims his one shot—
for I have heard him speak.
Seek my face, he has said.
And I can see myself now
with a detective, a sketch artist,
recalling his height, build,
age range, hair, skin, eyes,

chin, nose, cheeks, forehead.
Through cloudy bits of data
I am perceiving him.
I see him now in court.
I listen while he testifies,
gives evidence, makes the case
for his defence, his prosecution.
I sit across from him now,
his visitor behind glass.
Find him, he says. *Find him.*

Let him come to me. Let me
be the person he shatters
like a mirror. Then let it go dark
all around us. Then let the dark
gather together. And then let light
reconstitute. Let sight
start again. Let his sentence
be the plain light of day
by which I see him. Before
he sits strapped and hooded,
buckling as the charge passes
through him, and he slumps,
let him and me start over again.
Let the story we tell together
be the one story there is to tell.
Let his crime be told
and then re-told the way a dream
is told by a mirror filling with light.
Let him turn and listen to me
when I beg him, *Find me. Find me.*

A Drop of Blood

The drop of blood
falling from the cut above a man's eye
is one drop.
That drop multiplies
when blood runs out of a man's spleen
and out the side of his mouth
while he lies stabbed on a street
and a pool collects beside him.
That pool widens
when several men are lined up
against a wall in another place and shot.
It widens further when bombs
are dropped on a city.
That drop continues to multiply
until it becomes a terrible dawn
reaching into every eye.
Now what we see
begins with that drop,
and the pulse propelling it
allows it to measure space.
In this sun
of flaring blood,
and on the earth
made of its pouring
backed-up shadows,
how can we begin again
carrying out radiant repair
in measuring what we do?
How can we make
infinite bandaging
for our always-opening wounds?

Wash our eyes in great light?
Do not explain to me
how a person can drown
in an inch of water.
Blood tells us
how we can all drown in a drop of blood.

The Chance

The chance is hard to find.
If you get the chance, you should kill yourself,
said the policeman to a man heading to prison.
And then: *Hungry? We can get you something to eat.*

I dreamt I cradled in my arms
a ragtag collection of sparks.
My arms were dark; the sky out the window was dark.
The breath with which I touched
the sparks and made them flow in a white circle
was without a name; the sparks were without a name.

It was the chance. The chance that might allow me
to collapse the walls around myself,
destroy the bitter hour. The chance that is the sleep
of light, the one dream. And is my only judge.
Stand up to yourself, the judge says, and die
while you still can in your little life.

Your life made of days and nights,
your outpost on more wanting than you can know—
if you get the chance, you should set it on fire.
With this first kiss you will feed the sun and stars.

II

Water Makes Its Way

I walk out of the apartment early in cold iron rain.
The avenues fall away into the inlet.
The rivers in the canyons drag rivers of mist.
Crows and echoing caws scrape past.
I go up a ravine trail. The waters of the creek
coming down through the boulders are bone bright in the pre-dawn
and display a pouring crush of skeletal remains.

I come back. I look in on them in their room.
My two small children are there sprawled
where they have overturned the bed covers and twisted free.
She is a flying girl with wrists of a pixie,
discovering mysterious signs on every tree.
He is a climbing boy grasping with ease
bar after horizontal steel bar and swinging in the sky.

Water makes its way through the pair of them
carrying beginnings within their limbs
as it does within sunlit quick-travelling clouds and stagnant mire.
It blesses, damns and owns all dreams.
It lies as ice and snow in the forest on the mountain,
it reveals itself in a thaw bringing
deep, unordered runoff. Let me be a good man.

Soccer Ball

When my young father drives a soccer ball
through the picture window of our house,
I hear the thwack and boom of the leather sphere against his boot,
I behold the window glass shatter from end to end
and the particles lift in a circular raying pattern
to re-form and manifest as a miracle in the air.

My mother is young and glittering-eyed,
and I dream she and my father love one another, and love me.
I have not yet pleaded that I never again wake in this house.
I study encyclopedia pages with photos of outer space. I read
a novel in which Tom Swift builds a rocket ship. I dream
of the map of the solar system on the wall beside my bed,
I say the names of the planets in order of their distance from the sun.

My father does it a second time. He turns and drives
the soccer ball through the new window pane. I am outside
in the front yard again and right beside him. It is happening again.
What I see defies all laws. I have not yet heard him break,
have not yet watched while he burns her with cigarettes,
have not yet run from my downstairs room out into the black street
to a door and a neighbour and a telephone, but glass
is shattering and is a brilliant wormhole opening in my chest.

I have not yet observed my father in his fury
circling around and around the morning lawn,
or the policemen arriving in flashing cars to take him away.
I have not yet stood there invisible, intact window glass,
glass that seems not to be there, glass you walk into
not seeing it, shattering it and harming yourself,
cuts across your face and arms, marked up in blood.

The house has not long since been torn down, it still stands,
the ball lost in it, and I am still standing there
in the front yard where only a few hours on a night
in the spring of my ninth year have passed,
when I am returned here again through the wormhole of glass

to where I have already lived more than half my life,
and am a father kicking a soccer ball on a field
with my four-year-old son, who is almost too young to play,
and keeps picking up the ball. *Remember, in soccer
we don't use our hands,* I repeat. And then he shows me
how he can dribble the ball, and control it, with his little feet.

Teeth

Tooth enamel is different from bone. When bone breaks it heals itself—it makes a callus and immediately begins growing new bone. But when my father's father lay in his care facility bed the day before he was to die, he lay where his bones had shattered within the sack of his ninety-year-old flesh and stayed that way. *My son!* he said, shaking his head and gritting his teeth. *My son!* His teeth frightened me—his teeth harder and more brittle than bone. When tooth enamel breaks, or a rent develops in it, it cannot repair itself, no new enamel will replace it, and the living pulp of blood vessels and nerves hidden within it will shriek in its little abyss like a desperate ghost. My grandfather's teeth frightened me. They were not living tissue, they were phosphate, non-living while he was alive, and now as morphine loosened his tongue in front of me I saw his teeth loosen and leave his mouth and begin a new existence apart from him. His teeth presented themselves to me like my rightful inheritance, like a bequest. *My son!* he uttered again, louder, staring and unable to focus his eyes, his voice making its way out through the teeth that now confused him. He did not want to see me there at his bedside. He wanted to see his son. Or did he think I was his son? What a bequest! *My son!* If only I had been his son! That intelligent! That charismatic! If only I had been his son! I almost confessed to my grandfather right then—I had tried for half of my life to pass myself off as a facsimile of his son. I had tried. It had been a kind of dying—like living an afterlife before I lived. But my teeth—so much of the pulp scooped out for posts and gutta-percha—as terrible as they were, were my own, and not my father's, and not afflicted with periodontal disease. The false teeth in the middle of that handsome face! My teeth were my own! If only I could grant my grandfather his dying wish. *My son!* he repeated. All his teeth had now uprooted themselves out of his mouth. My grandfather's teeth had abandoned him. His teeth were now transforming into clacking spirit. He rubbed his gums together, saliva flowing, spraying. *My son!* What a bequest! But it was not a bequest. It was a condemnation. With his naked gums, he was cursing me for not being his son. Or was he cursing who he thought was his son? Here I was, a fully grown man, and as afraid of him and anxious to please him as I had ever been. But this was the moment I felt my own teeth hold in their supporting structure. This was when I heard myself say, gritting my teeth, *My son!* If my teeth had been a shovel, they would have been a steel alloy shovel with a blade able to bite through and dig deep into the dark carbon of life. My own son's adult teeth—they would be a power shovel, a shovel that would drive like a jackhammer. But they would never be like the jackhammer that I held horizontal as a teenager on my first job, doing what I was told by a boss who wanted to see me rip my palms apart on the chisel—never be like the jackhammer that made me think of my father and his jobs in my grandfather's factories, and my grandfather able but unwilling to hire me when I myself was looking for work. My own son's teeth pushing through the gums—his unstopping incisors! My teeth healthy and strong in my offspring! My teeth! My son's teeth! The father of fathers who is no one but my son—his adult teeth coming in holding the power of the dead and the living. The darkness within them, concentrated within the shining white enamel! His teeth like those of an exceedingly fine young Egyptian prince, like forms of light manifesting out of the dark—the light in the possession of no one except him, the light arriving streaming through the dark within his thick little cock, the light pouring through the Lego pieces of the buildings he constructs and that house my lost grandfather and father. *My son! My son!* What we cannot know is what we most are.

Tying Shoes

When my father's shoelaces come untied, I do them up—
and he is unaware I have been there.

I kneel in my life to tie my own shoes,
I see him struggling to reach down, to work his hands,

I tie my shoes and his at the same time—
and so it occurs: with his laces I make knots and bows appear

like performing magic using my thumbs and fingertips,
like playing a virtuoso solo on a stringed instrument.

I have cursed him: cursed him for cuffing me on the head;
cursed him for kicking me repeatedly down a flight of stairs,

remembering his suede boots hitting my back and stomach—
then gone on to wear that style of boots myself.

I tie his shoes for him now, and I see him in an elsewhere:
I imagine him having come through time

released into joy, and into endless old age;
he knows no bodily pain, his hands neither stiffen nor shake

as they might have done in old age here,
they simply bewilder him as they go useless—

and now he finds he has done up his shoes easily,
and he is like a little boy who has just learned how,

and feels pleased and praised that he has passed this milestone—
but it is me, I am the tier of his shoes, I am his son.

Question

Her shoulder blade. Wing bone of a wren.
Six years old, thirty-five pounds. After her
bad dream that she cannot remember,
her running to the *big bed*. Her falling backward
from a tree, and me running carrying her
to the hospital. Her on the playground
alone and yearning for a friend.

Nothing given for me to see can be
more than this, and yet the nameless love
that allowed her to arrive in my eyes
can only be blind to what it brings into being.
It has always already continued on.
The hand that fashioned her shoulder blade
and left her here with all it has created

is almost visibly drawing curved lines
through the air like pathways between
darkness and light, silence and singing.
And the inflamed nerve that stops me
as I turn to try to answer her question—
Daddy, how does a leaf know to fall?—
lights a travelling fire that hooks

through my shoulder. Even her question
sends me trying to rescue her,
and when I hear a voice saying *Farewell*,
I realize it is myself, vanishing; I know
that when she dies I will not be there to grieve—
and my daughter is a song and I am a leaf
that falls and watches itself fall.

My Four-Year-Old Son and a Bicycle Pump

Snoring while he lies curled up beside me,
the breath going in and out
through the vibrating contraption of his nose, mouth and throat—
he is in total contentment after uproarious play
and the big lunch I made him of a grilled cheese and a smoothie,
and immediate head-sinking-into-the-pillow,
eyelid-plummeting sleep,
probably dreaming of Lego, R2-D2,
his set of plastic tools, his collection of cars and other vehicles,
maybe, who knows, even his ABCs.

This snoring, this rhythmic near-chuckling
to himself must be part
and parcel of this pleasure-filled slumber—
the crazy hard right, hard left detours of his inhaling and exhaling
like his jokes he himself laughs at right through
(*What happened when the alligator died? The computer started to work.*
Why did the policeman crash his car? To eat an instruction.)—
and unbeknownst to him, it renders me
unable to sleep at all, and as I listen
to the sound of his obstructed breathing

I follow a route in myself to a garage
where it is fifty years ago and I am four
and working the handle of a manual bike tire pump as tall as me
while my father squats and holds the rubber hose
so that the airflow blows in my face and makes me laugh hysterically.
I am at the pump in the garage
adjacent to the house of my father's father, where mounted on a wall
is a bicycle hand-built by my great-grandfather,
brought to Canada from the old country
decades before I was born. I am laughing,

and laughing now closed-eyed while I watch myself,
and although it is said that joy
has no father or mother, I am thinking
that my moment with my father is the forebear of my son's happiness.
And I imagine he will carry
this happiness within him and one day
pass it down through the generations—
but at present he simply snores, working the air
as if he is at a bike pump, and steering through a nap,
dreaming the turnings of the wheel of his life.

Copper Door

To drive by his house is to look from the street
up beyond the low stone wall and the slope of lawn
to the rectangle of reddish-orange glow,
the copper door covered with the hundred indentations
of his workman's hammered decoration.

The door would open and come to a quiet close,
unlike the old man who died in pain, his bones crumbling
within him where he lay in his care home bed
uttering a metallic growl through gritted teeth.

To drive by at random once in a year or two—
is to see that the new owners have let the once-smart place go,
the exterior of the house badly in need of fresh paint,
the yard patchy with dirt and yellowed tall grass
and straggling shrubbery, all of it unsightly.

To knock on the front door of this house now
would be to see his work close up, to touch the metal
with a toddler's hands, and hear the opening
and closing of the copper-clad entranceway as soft
as my decades-dead grandmother's accented voice.

It would be to say to the current owners, *Hello,*
I am the eldest grandson of the man who built this house.
I did not know him well—his son and my mother
parted when I was a boy—but I know this door.

It would be to smell copper—the smell familiar to me
as it must be to a miner in Chile or Peru,
or as it must have been to men who first worked with copper

millennia ago—though I know now,
the smell would not be the metal, it would be oxidation,
the oils of human skin meeting copper and changing in air.

Perhaps when the house is finally torn down,
the copper of the door will be recycled, and reappear elsewhere—
for whereas my grandfather was never to come back,
except in a son, and in that son's sons, in a surname,
the copper, the Cu, atomic number 29, unalterable,
with which my grandfather sheeted the door of his house,
will stay itself always, its purity its only address.

Perhaps one day, I and the other men who have gone through
the door that was my grandfather into our passing lives
will arrive at a house where each of us is his own door
that opens on our first selves, fundamental together,
and where what we touch is what we remember
and has the touch on it of the dead and the living.

Dandelions

On the anniversary of my grandmother's death,
I am given a lesson in music. I learn my heart muscle
contracts in a rhythm unbroken with her last pulse-beat;
her heart's rhythm was a continuation
of a far-flung succession of pulse-beats.

I am given a lesson in art. I learn my grandmother
paints in colours she gathers from the spring sun,
and draws with these early April rays—here is the stroke
of her brush in her great-granddaughter's brass curls
so unlike the straight black hair she herself had as a child;
here is the sweep of her sketching pencil
in a playground where her great-granddaughter practises
pumping her legs and swinging straight and high on her own.

I am given a lesson in dandelions. Now I learn
my grandmother points with her great-granddaughter's finger
to a dandelion in a parking lot, a flower head
with its numerous ray florets—an Irish daisy,
a set of lion's teeth, a wild endive—a sprig of yellow sun;
then points to another, this one a seed head,
the plumes of all its seeds a white gossamer ball—
a witch's gowan, a down-head—a galaxy.

Here is my daughter forgetting all else running
to the sphere of the mature flower. With her breath
swinging on her heartbeats she disperses the delicate stars
over long, long distances, filling dark spaces
and filling my grandmother's eyes. I learn
these eyes help set the bound of the travelling seeds,
and hold us, my child and me, within the circumference

of the dandelions that will spring up again next year.
I see how my grandmother shows her great-granddaughter
her face in the clock of the dandelion, and how
as my daughter counts the number of puffs it takes
to blow the seed filaments from the dandelion,
my grandmother teaches my daughter to tell time.

Picking Blackberries with My Daughter

We discover together a long bramble wall,
and come back on half a dozen days in August

to where there is blackberry after blackberry
for me to put in the container I bring and for her to put in her mouth.

Is it okay to pick the red ones? Is that a bee?! Is it?!
No, it's not a bee, it's a wasp, I tell her. Bees, wasps—don't be afraid.

My three-year-old picks and picks until she's tired
and asks me if we can go home. My container is full.

The countless blackberries left—for sparrows, raccoons, squirrels,
for the air into which the fruit rots away.

Will the blackberries be here again?
Yes, they'll be here again, I say. They'll vanish and reappear—

they'll arrive, they'll go, they'll come back
through their places in the bramble,

they'll travel from this blackberry bush to this blackberry bush.
It's a sorrow bush. It's a joy bush.

Can we come back here again?
Yes, we'll come back, I answer. In my way I pray we will.

We'll come back like people with prayer notes,
and we'll fill our hands again with blackberries.

They'll stain your lips, tongue, chin and cheek with their juice,
they'll explain you like the wine that you will one day drink.

Whatever we ask for, whatever words we use,
the blackberries will be here, like prayers that grow in empty spaces.

Xmastime Dancing

The day of the longest night of the year,
two children are giving an impromptu performance
in the Lynn Valley Centre shopping mall
where a man is playing a piano. The girl
doing her ballerina moves, stepping lightly,
wafting her arms like a fairy, the boy
doing his martial arts moves, slashing the air,
or breakdancing, dropping down on all fours,
trying to kick out a leg. I feel my chest
tighten on a sudden darkness inside. It is real,
death is this close, and is nothing if not joy. The night
is almost here, and my little kids dance
in the dazzle of the enormous lit-up tree
and the glow of the decoration-strung shopfronts.
Song after song, they dance. And this is when
two elderly people holding onto each other
come hobbling out of the dim margins of the mall.
It is my grandparents, here where they would once walk in
every day at the same time and find a table
and have the seniors' lunch special. They have come back,
they have followed the electric current
along the never-ending looped pathway
of a circuit and arrived at snowflake stars
and a bright space where my kids move hypnotized
by "Jingle Bells" and "Rudolph the Red-Nosed Reindeer"—
and the living world is strange to them now
but warm and exquisite, as a food court meal
was once a banquet. They try to touch the sounds of the songs.
They stand here carefully. And they watch while a seven-
and four-year-old dance wildly. My grandmother
wants to join these children who seem familiar.

My grandfather feels the urge to snap bad photos
with a film camera. They know they must return
to where they have travelled from, and know the way
will be long and last the night, and that this is right—
still, they almost step out onto the radiant floor.
Now my grandmother reaches and briefly takes hands
with both children. Now she and my grandfather
turn and disappear, and my kids continue to dance.

Woolly Snow

We wake to a surprise of snow.
When it is time to leave for kindergarten,

she is in the middle of a drawing.
Outside, our car is layered thickly in the white,

and snow comes down to cling to my sweater
and cover the pocket in which I put her crayon.

If I forget my quick morning promise
to the artist of what is called "Woolly Snow"

that I will keep it and take care of it—
and she will be able to continue her work

with exactly the same special crayon
when she is back home in the afternoon—

the snow falling all day and for one day
in late spring when snow never falls

will make me think again of what I said to her,
flakes spinning, giving me soft clothing,

and arriving in her picture like a lamb
of the new air coming to be shorn.

III

The Shore

They sit or lie in a crowd on the shore,
all waiting themselves out. Among them
my father. If he recognizes me,
he does not acknowledge it. Only leers
at and past me, traces of glittering
in his otherwise empty eyes. The face,
the once beautiful man's face, keeps changing,
displaying different masks of filth and rot.
His voice half animal shriek, half grinding,
he offers me a drink of vanilla.

This is when a man not me hurls himself
out of my frame, and I bow. I reach out,
touch his shoulder and feel a brilliance sing
through me, and now know what I serve. The man
of light vanishes, but there is a wind
circling in the men on the shore, the breath
I drew as mine when I touched him. To leave
here I must follow what there is of him
shining and flitting over the dark waves
on into the darkness in front of me.

Bubble

A library of birds lifts away from a tree—
birds of every call number, they go,
acquisitions to be shelved in an instant
within new rows of summer leaves.
A block away on top of a high-rise
under construction, a crane spins
slowly half around, shifting the sky.
A seagull, a concentrated white cloud,
does a dipping glide, the distance
between me and my dead. I am sitting
at a bright window and looking out
across the city hall courtyard. A small boy
pads by on a scooter, my grandfather
come back for the afternoon. A hunched
elderly man moves by with a cane,
helmeted like a playground kid.
A crow thrusts by, a ragged black rip
in the air. The crane spins again,
a mechanical dinosaur. In the courtyard
a half-dozen bicycles, just invented,
sit locked in stalls in the sun. A squirrel
races back and forth between a point A
and a point B. The crane spins again,
its great hook carrying a blown bubble
containing the city's meeting place.
The crane stops, and the bubble bursts,
and we are somewhere far, far away
which once required a hundred years
or more of travel, and the words in all
our books have been altered for a new past,
and we have not moved an inch,
and the birds of another tree have flown.

Tiny Crabs

Playing on a cold beach with my son,
I rolled over a large, heavy rock,
staggering backward with the effort.
He shrieked when he saw the crabs all flee
the hollow strung with unearthly slime
that was their home. Then briefly the sun
shone down hard on that dark little world,
then lessened, and there was only sand.

It was as when someone dies and you
spend your life pretending to be him,
or a person you have imagined,
and you hold on to your pretending,
and who you were in the time before
suddenly becomes unknown to you,
an absence that he made, a nothing
where you stare afraid, and where you run.

North Vancouver

I

I was born in the Lions Gate Hospital, in North Vancouver. While I was still in the womb, my sixteen-year-old mother paraded me up and down Lonsdale Avenue, the main street that runs where the log chute built by Jack Lonsdale once stretched straight down the side of Grouse Mountain all the way to the old Moodyville mills near the water.

II

I could not yet see the trees, or the lit falling rain, or the clouds touching the trees and houses, or the waters of Lynn Creek or the Seymour River, or Burrard Inlet with downtown Vancouver on the other side of it, or out to the Georgia Strait, or the hoisted hulls in the shipyards, or the row of grain elevators; I could not yet hear the cargo and bulk carrier ships' horn blasts travelling across the inlet and up into the windows of the houses and apartments, or the trains shunting all night along the shore.

III

The trees and the industry that grew from the trees had permitted my parents and grandparents to live here, and me to be born here, and when I was born, and the umbilical root severed, I would say now that I was ushered raw into the rain-lit air like a harvested tree that would have its branches sawn off, its body scaled, and be sent down to the mill to be cut into cedar shakes.

IV

I would say that the image in which I was made was a North Vancouver tree, and so the place I stood and sank my prayer was nowhere but in the trunk of a cedar or fir, a tree that went into planks, two-by-fours, plywood and the old wooden house I lived in briefly, the wooden stairs I climbed—I sank my prayer and offered up what I was while people built more and more houses bigger and bigger and higher and higher up the mountainsides, bringing cars like moving briefcases, removing the trees to make their views come true, and rain washed away layers of the surrounding soil.

V

Because I am from North Vancouver, trees, creeks, rivers and rain are my unconscious and my conscious self, and I can be nothing more than what I call this place, or what this place may have been called by those who created the first footpaths through the trees. Lonsdale, Seymour, Lynn—these names disappear in the rays of the morning sunlight falling between forest treetops.

VI

I have read that there is a tree of life connecting heaven and deep earth, and it has a name, but because I am from North Vancouver and must wonder what creeks, rivers, trees and rain were named before, and before, wonder whether a tree can ever keep a name other than *tree*— the way the first people here call themselves *people of the inlet.*

VII

The more years that go by, the more names I have learned leave me, the more the number of names I would like to learn increases—and I learn *Chay-chil-whoak Creek*, *Kwa-hul-cha Creek*, and then these names too gather like mist, then move off and away like mist.

VIII

The old-growth trees are gone, logged long ago, gone, and I will never see those trees, but the trees rising in rain and branching with all names in their arms, the trees standing here now, I belong to them, and whatever name I have been given, because I was born here I have been given a chance to forget this name beneath the lifting rain of the trees.

When the Rain Comes

When the rain comes, it is here to see us
and is here to see the bones of the dead in the earth of cemeteries
and the ashes of the dead scattered wherever they may be scattered.

I will tell it, and tell it, and tell it, and tell it,
I heard a voice say as I was waking from a dream of rain.

When the rain arrives, it is light falling,
cups of light beyond number falling, shattering and becoming
       raindrops—
baby steps of water that lead light away and away.
I will tell it, and tell it, and tell it, and tell it.

When the rain comes, light falls and bathes in its change,
it cries out in a touch, and the rain lifts and is still
and is a conception as visible as all that is lit, and is a perfect surprise—
I will tell it, and tell it, and tell it, and tell it.

When the rain comes, it brings with it
the past of someone I loved and who is gone,
and when the rain comes, it opens arms broken and waiting—
the rain of these arms can never open the same way twice.

When the rain arrives, the burning light
that falls as rain and that turns us to ash
reveals to us that what we will become
is what we see around us, and always it reveals this for the first time—
I will tell it, and tell it, and tell it, and tell it.

When the rain comes, when the touch of the rain arrives,
it is here to touch back to itself through us,
and is here to let us be its mirror, and what we show
is nothing but ourselves arriving at mirror after varying mirror—
I will tell it, and tell it, and tell it, and tell it.

When the rain comes, water looks back at the light
that brought it here to see us, the way I mistake
my fingers for another's hair, or my mouth for another's mouth of rain,
and that person vanishes into light, when the rain comes.

Cart Riders

I

Here in a clearing in a triangle of bush
wedged between a shopping mall and a thoroughfare,
at the side of a thin, rust-coloured stream,
men come with shopping carts and halt in a circle.
None of them carries a key to a home,
yet this place is like a lockable room,
a conclave from which all others have been expelled.
After bins, and bottle- and can-picking,
they enter a seclusion within bramble walls.
What looks for and finds them now is the rain.

II

The fearless, lit ones among them, who ride,
go with their carts down the long, swerving slopes
of North Vancouver, bombing the mountainsides
at seventy kilometres per hour, burning shoe rubber.
Every apparatus of sense in the riders
so quickened, as the small wheels of the carts
rattle and ring struggling to grip asphalt,
the riders hear the smallest far-off sounds,
and riding this fast are unseen, like pure spirit,
ready to become nothing but the rain.

III

The cash obtainable at the recycling depot!
The wine at the Capilano Mall liquor store!
To listen to the men in their circle of speech
is to hear a chant—the words running lost
along gums like the stream along its bed
while jaws shake like loose swivel casters and axles—
deadened every moment by traffic din,
the gas-engine vehicles speeding past. The chant
is taken up in seagulls' and crows' cries,
and now it is that of the falling rain.

IV

Who will drive his cart straight to paradise?
Who will know God in the air rushing against him?
The wild wheels jingle like skeleton keys.
The smoke from the ragged cardinals' fires
announces decisions—streets they will try.
The keys of their edged hearts open the sky.
Those same keys lock secrets deep within crimes.
Today they wake to ride. The Michelangelo
ceiling above them, the clear, washed blue, the brightness.
All that will ever arrive is the rain.

Sirens

Fire engines, police cars, ambulances—
they go by day and night near where we live
up the lane from the corner triangle
of fire hall, police station, hospital.
We hear every siren disrupt the air
like it is inside our front room. It all
excites my small son. The bright red as well,
the silver, the black, the white—together,
sounds and colours are for him the single
language of what brings wonder. Now something
is going on right on our block. My son
runs to the high window, steps with startling
precision onto the baseboard heater
cover, tries to climb the ledge, the rigging
of the blinds. Wild attention in his eyes,
he points, utters his urgent not-yet words.
He wants only to hear the vehicles,
the outsized versions of three of his toys,
see them speed to a stop across the street,
then see the firefighters jump to the curb
in their boots, helmets, goggles, hooks and ropes.

I am no brave, strong, wise Odysseus,
I am a man in an old apartment
paying bills, rent, electricity, food,
to keep my son, his sisters, his mother
and myself merely afloat. What I hear
in the street is no alluring high song;
it is the repeating instant of fear
blaring the emergency through my hours—
our building a roar of flames, no escape,

dire sickness, earthquake, us without supplies.
I am no ancient sailor manoeuvring
past the cliffs and rocks of an island shore,
yet everyone and everything I love
can appear far away and lost to me,
and an instant can tempt me to ruin.
And I hold my son so he will not fall.
And I hold to him. I kiss him, breathe in
the miracle smell of his hair, his skin,
keep the side of my head pressed against his
so neither of us will feel the alarm,
only the peace flowing within his skull.

And I am tied to him, and he to me,
our arms encircling while the vehicles
arrive in numbers and the sirens' sounds
swirl close, louder, louder now, terrible—
he and I act as a ship's mast that holds
a sail that fills with wind and steadies us
on the sea waves winding around the world.

Aftermath

Aftermath of immense battles
between the ocean and the sun,
the rainclouds come in darkening
with the shadows of crow feathers.
In the steep ravine, the raucous
new skeletons of the spring creek
fall together to a tunnel
going under a thoroughfare.
Then on the flat in its last run
to the mouth and the deep inlet,
the creek slides full and quiet past
the old Squamish cemetery,
white-painted wood crosses tilting
as if trying to see through trees.

It is called Wagg Creek, but that name
is not the name given to it
long before anyone named Wagg
existed, or his ancestors
dreamt of this far place. Few know how
to say the original name;
fewer know what the name might mean.
With melting mountain snow, with rain,
there is runoff; with water, air—
mist; and at all times, the creek-work
that continues to play beneath
the senses and traffic noise
and condo construction noise. The rain
must search for the lost creek it feeds.

The mists that gather at the mouth
move along the creek like the sloughs
that once arrived with the high tide.
Fishless sloughs of the lower sky,
they flow in lit, they bring mirrors
that they hang in the creekside bush
and the long, overhanging tree
branches, in the loosening crooks
of the unsheltered wood crosses,
in the separated outstretched
arms of the tumbling bone—they bring
what is not here but still displayed
in the vaporous surfaces,
in bright depths beyond the brightness.

If the mists could give living form
to what they showed, a grey heron
would lift through the creek and be seen
until it saw a car. A man
wearing a woven cedar hat
would appear where the ravine ends
at busy roads and built-out properties,
and see no path along the slough
and no way into the ravine;
he would be trapped in the dark gaps
in the creek waters' memory,
and have to stand and burn away
as it is always said mist will
in weather reports for the day.

At Safeway

Here is an elderly lady
asking the whereabouts of the liquid laundry soap.
She has been waiting in line just to ask.
Aisle 2, says the checkout girl.
The elderly lady heads off toward Aisle 4.
An elegant, tattered puppet, there she goes.
Excuse me, I call out to her. *It's over that way.*
The checkout girl leaves her cash register,
goes to the lady, guides her to the right aisle.
The lady disappears down Aisle 2.
Ah, getting old, says the man in line behind me.
Yeah, adds the woman behind him.
All of us waiting to pay for our groceries—
Did you find everything you were looking for today?
the checkout girl asks us in turn.
We wait for the elderly lady,
dividers in place, empty space
readied on the conveyor for her soap.
But where is she? The checkout girl
leaves us again to go look. Where is she?
Our eyes fix on the magazine racks,
taking in who is engaged to whom
(proposal made at a rented-out stadium),
who has gotten married, who has "hooked up,"
the photos of all the celebrities
who have found what they were looking for.
Is the elderly lady going down her aisle,
on either side of her the lit-up rows
of the many liquid laundry soaps
that will make her clothes clean and bright,
that will allow the dust to fall from her?

The checkout girl hurries back to us,
re-opens her cash register, dumbfounded,
having found no one. For a moment
before she picks up an item to scan,
she pauses, and together we wait for this lady
and are wedding guests awaiting a bride.
I see our elderly one casting off
her death clothes as she prepares for the ceremony,
washing in the dazzle and flow of a stream
clear as crystal, putting on new garments
of light and going safely to her groom of light.

Now, after we move dividers,
fill spaces on the conveyor,
utter club card numbers, insert debit cards,
give and take bills, collect shiny, dark-edged
coins tumbling out of a metal box into a cup—
Do you need help out? No, I'm fine, thanks—
we grab our groceries, say goodbye,
we leave and go out into the broken
aisles of the large parking lot, the streets,
the sidewalks, each of us mortal again.

Stopping the Waves

Here on the shore, he looks up at me and says he is a *guard*.
He is erecting a special structure.
In front of him, mist off the Pacific,

and the sun visible only along a line of melting chrome.
The waves slide in, smooth wavelengths, and low crests
with clusters of diamonds showing through coal.

This morning, gravitational waves and a less-than-a-second-long sound
were detected arriving at Earth.
A billion and a third years ago

two black holes each thirty times the mass of the sun
collided and merged and created energy
that rippled through the space-time of the universe to the earthly now.

Here on the shore, my small son is at work,
single-minded in his four-year-old way, in a trance like an odd tantrum.
He goes to the inlet edge, looks out at the mist

then down at the crushed glass froth and clear tidewater touching his
        shoes,
then out at the rows of waves, the proofs of every prediction,
then turns back to the January-cold, grey sand.

What is it? I ask. *It's to stop the waves,* he says. *I'm going to trap them.*
He seems to know what he means. What he means escapes me.
He is at work searching for his *lumber,* as he calls it.

And then I see. At high tide the waves will fill it. They will fill
his ragtag structure made of sticks and ocean-worn log scraps.
Little unknown man here on the shore,

he is building his trap as a shelter for the tide. And like any shelter,
it is an observatory; he will identify every kind of wave.
Now he is revealing to me his plan—his gates, doors, rooms, windows.

And like any shelter, it is himself. He is collecting the scattered pieces
of himself as he finds them along the beach, the right driftwood
that began travelling here before he was born. And for a few moments

with his elaborate device he will stop the waves
and display the cedar and olive, the gold, silver and copper within a
        temple,
and whatever was out there will have come this close,

though the waves will bring down almost all of the wood and depart,
and he will have to wait here on the shore as if he has always waited—
for new evidence, new instructions to rebuild given long, long ago.

Wildfire: Photos

Light laying out a new dead field.
Drought level 3, drought level 4—
smoke floating across a lake, fire lurching down a hillside

of homes: instead of the invisible wall
separating a town from fire, an immense off-the-grid
face revealing itself close up. It is now

that residents rush to find photos—
old volumes spilling prints, colour, black & white;
they are grabbing what is left in stone-lined pits.

Extended families, forebears,
are the millet sown in spring and harvested in summer,
the wheat and barley sown in fall and harvested in spring—

it is now that the suddenly starving eat,
feed the slow-burning carbon of their cells,
unroll the old film there like a prophecy. Homeless,

they turn their faces to rain, the film develops,
and they dream the albums they could not save,
the golden grasses, the storehouses full of grain.

Stroller

The hot late summer light
lies down in a stroller
in the form of a child
outside for the first time,
and the child gazes back
at the flow of the sun
beyond the canopy.
Hands to their brows, people
shade their eyes from the glare.
In a tall tree, the leaves
lift, and spin sparkling spokes.
A piano set up
outside for anyone
to play keeps the fall rain
in its keys. My children
grow, new grades calling them
from the one September.
I wait there already
where I will pick them up
again at three o'clock.
When the school buzzer goes,
it startles me awake
where I have closed my eyes
to feel a playing field
of great light. Then I turn,
and while it beats in time
to the shouts, wheel my heart
on a church truck of bone
to the flung-open doors.

The Water and the Stone Trap

In the creek gliding clear green and rippling white against rocks, the work of the water is to gather all the rocks and touch them completely and make them smoother and smoother, and take away layer after layer and offer this up to the inlet. The work of the rocks is to gather all the water, the way the people here once gathered fish after silver-scaled fish. The rocks collect the water, and the water collects the rocks—there is nothing else for either the water or the rocks. There is nothing else for what I call myself when I look and look at the creek, and my only thought is that I want the water to smooth me and take away layer after layer of me and allow me to travel in the flow, and usher me into the deeper, wider water of the sea. It is now that I know the work as if it is my own, this work of melted mountain snow and rain runoff and rock-rich glacial till down through the thousands and thousands of years. It is now that my eyes forget me, water and rocks gathering and gathering, and my eyes take me to be caught in a stone trap set in the creek, then to be gathered in the evening in a basket woven from cedar bark. That gathering is what I imagine will occur at the moment of my death, when I am stranded, and I gasp while I learn to breathe the element that is the other life, that is the love before what we know of love—the water and the stone trap will touch, and then the newly caught fish will be carried out under the black sky, funnelled into the basket of the stars.

IV

Birthmark

This morning as I woke,
the summer sun, the deep day, the brown earth—

all began with my memory of the mole
you carried on the inside of your thigh.

You are gone; I am lightly riding to my own death.
Once you asked if you should have it removed,

but a mole such as that one, I said, you should let stay.
Now it is my birthmark.

Two Houses

The house I ran from is gone. A new house stands where it stood.
I will never be able to go to that first house
as I have imagined I would one day

and ask the owners if I might intrude
and walk around the front room
and go down the staircase to stand in my old room.

The rock wall at the end of the backyard is not gone,
though it is held together only by crumbling mortar and vines.
Once I saw a rat run up the rockery

into a small dark gap, and disappear—
I stood watching with a hole in my forehead
made by a boy who hurled a stone at me from down the lane.

A house a block away is not gone. It was older,
much older than our house. This is the house I ran to.
The street I ran along was vast, the darkness vast—

it narrowed to an enclosed front porch,
where I knocked as I had at every house.
I could go to this house again,

but the mild couple who brought me inside and made a call
would be gone. They would be long dead.
The house, so well-kept, immaculate and fine an old house,

will likely still be here when I am dead
and not here to remember what only I can
of the book-lined den, the sweet smell of the baking. I am alive.

A Dove

A wild dove that has chosen the tree
outside our apartment for a home
flashes past with its lightning-white wings,
parts the vast curtain of green needles
in front of our window two floors up
and disappears. There is no olive
leaf in its mouth. Still, the apartment
shelters us like an ark, our quarters
inside its listing hull. There is rain
that comes sweeping against the glass, air
that turns purple-dark and storms that come
along with my dreams of my loved ones
lost forever. The dove reappears.
My two small children climb up to see it.
It as soon departs again—around
the side of the building, up above,
beyond our sight. There is the window
of our ark that lets in the sunlight.
The dove returns again, nothing
in its mouth but sunlight. All our eyes
must follow it, all our ears must fill
with its cooing. Its wings are the wings
we flap and flutter. The grey deluge
held in the world will rise around us,
and the wild dove arrive out of it
carrying our lives apart from us,
father, mother and child will be sent
to and from us by what is in us,
wing the way from the tree to the tree.

O God, Beast, Mystery, Come!

They will come edged in early running light,
brimming with blood, to see their arrows pierce
a stag, a muskox or horse, then let out their cry.
They will create paste from red clay ochre
and with it fill in the rhythmic outline of the animal
on secret torch-lit cave walls and ceilings.

I leave my life behind when a watercolour
of a palomino painted by my father leaves my hands.
On my school's gravel field I pin the boy
whose boot has trampled my picture, I lift
myself over him and bring my lunch kit
down like a machete across his face.

I take the throat of a boy who has taunted me
because I can run fast, run farther than the rest
without tiring; I seem to watch as I throw him
against the metal of a gym locker door
and clamp his throat there with my hands
to stop his breathing, until they pull me away.

I wait in the dark, I jump someone who jumped me
and hit him, fling him into a ditch, kick him
until he goes quiet, is unable to move; before
I hear the yelp of a siren around a corner
and veer off, I gaze at the palette of oils
in the moonlit muck splattered over him.

They will shriek, they will dance around a pit
where they have trapped a mammoth, never closer
to the life beneath the hide as when they spear it,
never closer to the energies of their fires
as when they push the fires into the pit and stare
at the burning creature that they will eat.

They will call their god, it will appear as a bull,
a snake with many heads, a lion with a mane of fire,
they will become it, dismember it in deep play,
while I will want my revenge; my enemy
will appear to me; my shout when I break him
to try to feel complete will break my face.

My crime be their crime, my return from the one
to the many; the crime of the one be my redemption.
Only the true criminal can forgive, and stand
in a chorus beside an eye nailed into an animal,
know the moment darkness and stars first touch,
the wild, careless joy in the steady song.

The Broken Face

There are blows in life, so powerful ... I don't know!
  —Cesar Vallejo, "The Black Heralds"

There are blows that break a man's face, and a white fire flames out—
when a judge strikes his gavel against a sound block and a charge is read,
a man's face breaks, a white fire flames out of it,
and the fire is all that is visible in the courtroom,
and is all that is beautiful, and it halts in the air, watching itself.

There are blows so powerful; the white fire accepts them,
it flames out as a face breaks and the face crumbles to sand;
a man's broken face is sand, and the fire that flames out of the face melts
        it,
and the man's face is glass; the court spectators look through it and are
        lost.

I listen as a man pleads his case—his crime is himself;
his crime can be nothing but himself, and his face can only break.
I hear him utter the last syllable of his plea and see his breath mist the
        glass,
see it paint it silver, and the glass of his face become a mirror.

The court arguments dirty the mirror, turn the mirror almost black.
No one can see anything in the blackened mirror—
this is what the proceedings reveal: the prosecutor and the solicitor
see nothing in the tried man's face; he sees nothing in his own face.

Still, the sound block must be struck; someone must be punished
for dirtying the mirror—for dirtying a face and all its reflecting
        substance.
Someone has to try to clean the mirror and clear himself.

There are blows that break a man's face. There are juries, judges—
they accuse a man of a crime, they deliberate, they convict, sentence,
they send a man to be received through prison doors.

There is the white fire that flames out of a man's face;
it hides the evidence of what it burns from beginning to end
repairing the man's broken face everywhere—
it imprisons itself in the man to try to see itself, it goes free
when the face breaks and the man must search and search for his face.

Summer Vineyard, Naramata

The noon sun reaches deep into the twining vines
and they cannot hold it, and the vineyard goes dark,
the dark of the wine waiting within the black grapes,
and this brings the foxes out of hiding—
white tail-tips giving off sharp musk and fluorescence,
they come bounding through the magnetic field
and ribboning and crisscrossing among the vineyard rows.
The small flowers in bloom, the foxes tear them
as they raid the vines, and the flowers scatter bright
and then disappear in the darkness like the sparks of the fires
that the sun has ignited in the foxes' tails
so that they will run carrying light. And they arrive,
and are a memory, as starlight is
of immense burning, as the smile of the wine is
of the wine. *Light, light, light*, say the foxes,
let there be weeping and burning, joy and burning.
Light the author of light, light its one word,
the light arrives and the vineyard goes dark.
Light, light, light, say the foxes as they burn
the vineyard like the hundreds Samson sent running
through the crops of his enemies, tying torches
to their tail-tips to burn the fields of standing grain.
They come now overthrowing the vineyard
and starving us with what we eat, making us thirst
with what we drink, they come ruining the blossoms,
they prepare a way for us, they wind through the vines
writing the name of light, and that is how they wait for us,
they wait though they cannot wait long enough,
they make us burn and wait for us while we burn, wait for us
to catch up, for our words to catch up, for love to catch up.

The Finch, Questions and Answers

What did the finch do?
It sang its song to the first words in your mouth.

What did the finch do then?
It dreamt its life in a strand of your hair.

What did it do then?
It stood in your upturned palm.

What it did do then?
It bathed in the bright waters of your forehead.

What it did do then?
It nested in the birthmark mole on the back of your hand.

What it did do then?
It flew your laughter out through your tears.

What did the finch do then?
It disappeared behind the grey-blue mirror of your eyes.

What did the finch do then?
It came back years and years later

and you lifted someone up to see it,
and you thought for both of us that it was me.

A Photograph

Those moments when you sat and spoke to me of how,
when an exquisite change took hold in us, you felt
that you were ugly, you could only whisper quickly, and you looked
        away.

But you did not look away for an entire night—
you stayed awake, the rest of the family asleep, you
alone in a room with your father. When light

came in with the morning air through a curtained window
and displayed an elderly man, mouth awry, eyes staring wide,
you stepped close and recorded it. With a slow

click you photographed him lying there curled up dead,
you collected the light like a disclosure.
Then you hid the photograph, and then you menstruated

for the first time in two years, the flow heavier
than any you remembered. You would not show it to me,
the white-bordered black & white, not to anyone, ever,

and not look at it yourself, the image of the strangely small body,
the loose belt allowing the robe to open and make visible
the withered penis that you could still see

being held out to you where he had told you to stand, and later kneel,
and later sit, on a chair. You would keep the photograph only
to keep it, like a secret gift that you had given yourself.

You go into that room of remembering now
by a route least likely to disturb evidence,
you note the way you entered the room—as if looking away.

You check for a sign of breathing, you check for a pulse
in the area of the neck. You note the time. You take in
every single detail you can. It is a case

in which you conduct the investigation
over and over, and conclude that you are a criminal. And you leave
certain that no one will ever learn of your self-condemnation

because you have hidden the photograph
where no one could possibly find it. And now
light is still its own clue, and beauty vanishes into its proof,

and the proof is called the world—and it is where you
exist like a hidden picture of yourself. The world may be made of lies,
yet the pure prayer in you to pure change is the one way

that I can know what is beautiful. Eyes
are to see in another's eyes what must conceal itself to search for us;
light is lost, light finds a path back to its beginning, and turning here,
        shines.

Girl on a Tire Swing

She remembers nothing
of how she came to be here—
the journey across continents and oceans,
the lying down in airplane aisles
shrieking and vomiting.

She remembers nothing
of her first language—
which let go its hold
and finally faded away within her
as she sat alone in front of the TV
mouthing the English
of video after video of *Winnie the Pooh*.

She tells me she wishes
she could remember.
It is all unknown to her—
the country of her first three years,
the meanings of the melodic
turnings of sounds in that other tongue,
the right way to say the name
she was given at birth.

When I see her now,
and speak with her
about her university courses
or her plans to travel soon
to far-off places,
I see her always on a morning
in a playground where I would take her,
and where she sat on a tire swing—

her five-year-old eyes
looking into the eyes
of a little boy who shared the swing with her;
his eyes looked into hers,
they went back and forth together,
they leaned into the sun,
and they were twin animals at play,
deep-sparkling, wild and miraculous,
being led on and on
somewhere they had never been,
but which was home.

The Wound

Follow the trail of the waves, the ocean says,
follow, and enter the circle of the ocean,
and come to what the waves come to continuously,
and say, *I need the sea because it teaches me.*

Thalassa! Thalassa! shout Greek soldiers
when they see the sea that tells them they are near again to their home.

Death, death, death, death, death, whispers the sea
out of a rocking cradle, whispering *the word up from the waves.*

Skaay the Haida stands here where the Pacific is circling,
the ocean with the spirit lodge on its floor,
the ocean in which *the roof planks ... flew,*
and *the crossbeams stood up on end and fell,* and *the rafters fell.*

Through the *sewn housefront* of his eyes at the ocean's brink,
Skaay sees the incoming wave—
he is here and he is sewing the surgical ridge
of the crest of the wave that hardens instantly
into thick scar tissue, and then breaks
and allows the wound of the beginning to widen beyond calculation.

The same wave and the same swift, glinting froth—
Shakespeare's soliloquies, his own *sewn housefront,*
Keats's odes, his threading his seeing heart
to the ocean's circling see-through blood,
his five senses helping to heal the wound.

The Pacific lies splayed in the sun.

The crest of each wave arrives at a rim of sand and at crime scene tape.

Come unto these yellow sands, and then take hands, sings a spirit.

Human beings tricked out of a clam by a raven—
those first human beings and the human beings now,
the s*urface birds,* they dance on the sand, they dance on the wild shore
that is the boundary between worlds.

They dance along ocean-encircling yellow crime scene tape.

They dance and they hear their dancing say,
I am part of the sun as my eye is part of me.
That I am part of the earth my feet know perfectly,
and my blood is part of the sea.

They dance as the ocean waves roll in and away
and collect up every wave that has ever rolled to the sand.

Like the ocean waves, the human beings dance,
and they hear their dancing say, *we die of the return-streaming of everything*
we have lived.

And into the circle, into the opening, closing, opening wound,
the universal womb of waters ...
the pure movement, the crystalline totality—
they release bitumen, polymers, effluent.

They find and they transport oil, and the oil spills
and soaks every grain of the sand lying along the rim,
and Blake sees in every grain every tanker ship
that ever has and ever will power its ocean-churning propellers down a
    coast.

Never, never, never, never, never, shouts Lear.

Now I am alone, cries Hamlet, and now his words
drown the stage with tears and cleave the general ear with horrid speech,
make mad the guilty and appall the free,
and amaze indeed the very faculties of eyes and ears.

Follow the trail of the waves, the ocean says,
follow, and enter the circle of the ocean,
and come to the Great Pacific Garbage Patch
filled with plastic, chemical sludge and debris
trapped by the currents of the waves of the North Pacific Gyre.

Follow the trail of the waves and come to what you have created.

You have sewn your own *housefront* and sewn the Pacific Trash Vortex.

You have stood here where Ghandl the Haida stands—
his tale all melodic repetitions and symmetries,
he is here and he is reciting his sequence
of magical tools for trading time and timelessness.

You have *travelled a ways* and travelled *a long way out to sea,*
where *a wren sang* ... and *punctured a blue hole* in a traveller's heart,
and with your own tools you have bound yourself with plastic.

And *through the feckless years* you return here again,
and you travel and return, and return always to the scene of the crime—
and you secure and process the scene, you gather the evidence
waiting along the sand, you produce a timeline, you investigate.

You put the entire ocean on your witness stand—
when the ocean has said what it has to say to you, when it has said
    everything.

I am the sea, I am the sea! repeats a poet singing of the mana of the sea.

The beating of the waves we hear when we hear our own pulse—
we have wrapped ourselves around a wave and held it
and formed our ear and now our ear is *a whirlpool fierce.*

We have wrapped ourselves around the ocean, and are fluttering crime
        scene tape.

Far out on the waves is a floating mass of tangling poisons—
it is our punctured heart we make a dirtier and dirtier mirror.

The opening, closing, opening wound, breaking, stitched, breaking—
is love freed again and again from anything that binds it.

The love in the *surface bird*, the desire in it for the other shore,
the other shore than has no shore—is the hunger of a gull
trying to flap wings oil-slicked or trapped in coils, and the waves circle
and the *surface bird* cannot lift itself from the sand.

Creating a Timeline

Be a detective.
Gather together details—maps, photos, names. Put it up on a wall.

Carry out an investigation
as a tortured chief of police

obsessed with a decades-old cold case file.
The deceased is far more alive for you

than anyone you can touch in the present.
If you find the right clues, and if you connect them,

you will have found the neutrino, the ghost particle—
which will let you send a message into the past.

Now you may finally tell her
what you feel for her, and know that she knew before she died.

On the possibility that she killed herself—
your message might deter her. It's true. We can alter the past.

And love—is an alternate reality. She strikes you
in a trillion ways every instant. She goes through you where you stand.

Is she to be mute forever? Look, you can see—
the forensics suggest she was trying to speak.

Be a theoretical physicist.
Build a detector to catch a ghost particle.

Build it underground in a gold mine,
in a tunnel beneath mountains, in an ocean, in Antarctic ice—

like early humans painted pictures
of bounding animals deep in caves.

Be a poet.
Say, *A sudden blow: the great wings beating still above the staggering girl*—

a god in his marauding desire
takes the form of a swan and assaults a girl,

and her fate rushes through her in multiple tragic historical events.
Blind eternity defiles her.

You see someone all the time—
though you are aware that the god of death gathered her up years ago.

Is she the ghost particle?
Are you? Are the two of you?

In the life she and you did not have together, there was a child—
you did not look past it and sweep it away before it could be born.

That child is creating your timeline, shifting the details,
uncovering the messages it writes to you one day.

Change

For two days the air is different, veiled.
No one mentions it. As if a censer is swinging
through the avenues. Thunder, lightning,
then an ecstasy of rain. And my children
and I sit in our second-floor apartment
in the power outage, and wait for the sound
of the next rock-splitting distant and as close
as within our skulls, the next flash of the sky.
An immense animal that might have arisen
on a bank of the Nile, its hide hard as stone,
its heart hard as a nether millstone,
is brushing up against the window glass.
The older child frightened yet excited,
the younger one laughing. Their eyes full
of nothing but the dark, the repellent sheen.
Everything about to change. The two of them
not long out of their mother's womb,
and me long out of my own mother's womb,
the three of us are clasping together
and making a single fetus sucking its thumb,
and what has arrived is now throwing itself
at the side of our apartment building
and making it shake like a rotted wood ship.
And now it is calling for us, wanting to play,
trying its voice against our eardrums,
the mouth wide open and hungry for us.
The wild atom of its face, no hook capable
of controlling it, is trying our beholding of it
against our eyes as it whips away, leaving
a shining wake. Our ears, our eyes, a trick,
a sleight of hand. Everything about to change.

Notes & Acknowledgements

The title "O God, Beast, Mystery, Come!" is taken from a speech in Euripides's *The Bacchae*.

The quotations in "The Wound" come from works by poets as follows: *I need the sea because it teaches me* (Pablo Neruda); *Thalassa! Thalassa!* (Homer); *Death, death, death, death, death ... the word up from the waves* (Walt Whitman); *the roof planks ... flew ... the crossbeams stood up on end and fell ... the rafters fell ... sewn housefront* (Skaay); *Come unto these yellow sands, and then take hands* (Shakespeare); *surface birds* (Skaay); *I am part of the sun as my eye is part of me. That I am part of the earth my feet know perfectly, and my blood is part of the sea* (D. H. Lawrence); *we die of the return-streaming of everything we have lived* (Galway Kinnell); *the universal womb of waters ... the pure movement, the crystalline totality* (Pablo Neruda); *Never, never, never, never, never* (Shakespeare); *Now I am alone ... drown the stage with tears and cleave the general ear with horrid speech, make mad the guilty and appall the free ... and amaze indeed the very faculties of eyes and ears* (Shakespeare); *housefront* (Skaay); *travelled a ways ... a long way out to sea ... a wren sang ... punctured a blue hole* (Ghandl); *through the feckless years* (Earle Birney); *I am the sea, I am the sea!* (D. H. Lawrence); *a whirlpool fierce* (William Blake); *surface bird* (Ghandl); *the other shore that has no shore* (Pablo Neruda); *surface bird* (Ghandl).

Many thanks to the editors of the publications in which some of the poems in this book first appeared: *Arc, The Dark Horse* (Scotland), *Event,*

FreeFall, Grain, Juniper, The Maynard, Prism, The Winnipeg Review. Many thanks to the Alfred Gustav Press, which published some of these poems in a chapbook, *Stopping the Waves* (2017), and a holm, *Aftermath* (2018).

And many thanks to Silas White and Nicola Goshulak for their extremely adept editing.

About the Author

Russell Thornton is the author of *The Hundred Lives* (2014),
shortlisted for the Griffin Poetry Prize, and *Birds, Metals, Stones & Rain*
(2013), shortlisted for the Governor General's Award for Poetry, the
Raymond Souster Award and the Dorothy Livesay Poetry Prize. His
other titles are *The Fifth Window, A Tunisian Notebook, House Built of Rain*
(shortlisted for the Dorothy Livesay Poetry Prize and the ReLit Award
for poetry) and *The Human Shore*. Thornton's poetry has appeared in a
number of anthologies, among them *Love Me True, Sustenance, Refugium:
Poems for the Pacific, In Fine Form, Best Canadian Poetry in English 2012,
Open Wide a Wilderness: Canadian Nature Poems* and *Rocksalt: An Anthology of
Contemporary BC Poetry*. His poems have been featured several times on
Vancouver buses as part of BC's Poetry in Transit. Thornton has lived
for extended periods of time in Montreal, in Aberystwyth, Wales, and
in Salonica, Greece. For the past number of years he has lived where he
was born and grew up, in North Vancouver.